T0195028

LaMont Erik Carter

authorHOUSE

AuthorHouse™
1663 Liberty Drive
Bloomington, IN 47403
www.authorhouse.com
Phone: 833-262-8899

© *2021 LaMont Erik Carter. All rights reserved.*

No part of this book may be reproduced, stored in a retrieval system, or
transmitted by any means without the written permission of the author.

Published by AuthorHouse 01/08/2021

ISBN: 978-1-6655-0973-2 (sc)
ISBN: 978-1-6655-0971-8 (hc)
ISBN: 978-1-6655-0972-5 (e)

Library of Congress Control Number: 2020924056

Print information available on the last page.

Any people depicted in stock imagery provided by Getty Images are models,
and such images are being used for illustrative purposes only.
Certain stock imagery © *Getty Images.*

This book is printed on acid-free paper.

Because of the dynamic nature of the Internet, any web addresses or links contained in
this book may have changed since publication and may no longer be valid. The views
expressed in this work are solely those of the author and do not necessarily reflect the
views of the publisher, and the publisher hereby disclaims any responsibility for them.

I AM A CHILD OF GOD; I am a man. I am a Black man. I am an American. I am an African Black American. I am an American soldier.

My name is LaMont Erik Carter. I was born on August 1, 1970, in West Jersey Hospital in Camden, New Jersey. My father is Russell Ralph Carter, and my mother is Betty Ann Danford. I have a brother, Jermane Desmond Carter, and a sister, Lakesha Erika Carter.

Today, I believe I have lived my life well, but I want to live my life to its fullest. The mission is to give you a sense of my life based on my view of my own experiences in the hopes that we will discover a camaraderie among ourselves. I am ready and full of faith that this is possible.

I spent my early childhood on 568 Spruce Street in Camden. When I think about strong experiences that had

a precise impact on my life, I always think about my family. From the beginning, my father's and mother's families were fortified in brotherhood and sisterhood. My uncles and aunts on both sides of my family forged these bonds from growing up together. I credit each one of them for providing me with a very strong family support system. From the time that my parents were married, the Carters and the Danfords easily became a strong and solid family. I grew up with my cousins as if we were brothers and sisters. But as time has passed, I have come to acknowledge that we have emotionally and physically grown apart as a family. Life has stretched my family in different directions. The struggles and trials of life have taken A toll on us. Does this sound familiar to you, brothers and sisters?

Mothers against fathers, fathers against sons, mothers against daughters, brothers against brothers, sisters against sisters, brothers against sisters ... this is the cycle! We can attribute our struggles to other factors, of course. We know what contributed to causing the damage to our family, so

let's begin with the repair. Change doesn't happen unless we start with ourselves; let's work on changing the narrative.

My early years in Camden were beautiful. I had a lot of brothers and sisters. Having family in all parts of Camden helped me feel very safe and secure. My family molded me into the man I am today. My father taught me how to be a man, and my mother taught me the characteristics of a strong and nurturing woman. Alongside my parents, my younger siblings taught me how to be a protector and how to be righteous. I am certain it is within our families that we initially develop the foundation for our character.

In 1982, I moved with my family to 15 Pembrook Lane, Willingboro, New Jersey—an address that was the beginning of a new environment for us. This relocation had a strong impact on my life. I had never cut so much grass in my life before I moved to Willingboro. There were parks, pools, and basketball courts in each neighborhood. There

were many different races and cultures: Blacks, Puerto Ricans, Indians, White, Chinese, Japanese, and others.

The Willingboro school system was excellent in my opinion, providing many electives and courses. We had classes in cooking, typing, woodshop, mechanics, pottery, and cosmetology, and we even had our own Willingboro High School television crew! It wasn't until the eleventh grade that I learned how to type, and I found a new interest. I got into the IT field in 1997, and it amazes me how learning to type on a typewriter in high school during a time when computers weren't even mainstream would be a necessary skill for a career I didn't even know I would pursue.

I have deep roots through my family in Camden. But I have deep roots through myself in Willingboro. Most of my lifetime bonds and friendships were established in Willingboro. Therefore, I recognize Willingboro as my hometown.

I consider myself to have been an average teenager. I didn't join the football, track, or basketball teams in school, and I was not at the top of my class academically, but my intelligence stood out. I was a very social person—I had friend groups with various connections, and I had a main group of friends. I believe my range of friendships was beneficial to meeting new friends. I developed more bonds by meeting people through friendships already established. I mastered this technique and still employ it.

Relocating to Willingboro had a strong impact on my life. My brother and I would think about the great times we shared in Camden, but we always agreed we were in the exact place we were meant to be: Willingboro, New Jersey.

After graduating high school in 1988, I joined the US Marine Corps in 1990. My military occupational specialty (MOS) was 0311 Infantry Rifleman. I participated in Operation Desert Storm and Operation Desert Shield. I

achieved the rank of corporal (E-4) and was honorably discharged in 1994.

My military service also had a strong impact on my life. I became a soldier. Most of my family members have served in the military at one time or another. Some experienced war and combat as I did. My father, whether he realizes it, prepared me for the marine corps. Like most soldiers who become fathers (including myself), he used training he received in the military as a benchmark for how he organized his household and children. This structure helped me adapt quickly to marine corps boot camp in Paris Island, South Carolina. I already understood authority. Then I learned how to follow. I learned how to follow plans. I learned that leaders are a collection of particularly good information. I learned that if this knowledge were used effectively, missions would be successfully completed. And ultimately, I learned how to be a leader myself.

The effects of war and combat increased my consciousness. The conditions of combat forced me to depend on my fellow soldiers. It was my military training that instilled this behavior in me. This is how I survived. I will not discuss war as glorious or victorious, but I will tell you that death and the dealing of it will always be a part of me.

Today, I see our world as a gift! We would not be part of it if this were not true. Everything in our world is a benefit to our lives. We are breathing its air, eating its vegetation, and drinking its water. Do you believe that our world was specifically and purposely created with the intention to support and nourish life? I have faith that you do. This knowledge is my perceived basis for our alliance. This will be our common ground as brothers and sisters. We are living because we are part of a living world. There is no other life discovered in our universe. Earth is the bank, and Earths most valuable and precious asset, compared to any other planet in our solar system, is life. How are we

spending our time on earth, though? We are spending our lives as if **life** is not valuable. We spend a lifetime trying to accumulate a very false sense of wealth. Let us attempt to resolve this error, this way of thinking small!

Our world is a miracle; we are a miracle. We are not a mistake, and we did not just happen to exist. There are precision movements involved in our creation. Earth is in just the right vicinity of our sun—perfectly placed, in comparison to all the other planets in our solar system, to sustain our life. We know this! Earth is a living planet. Besides human life, Earth has its own interconnected life growing from within. This interconnected life miraculously creates the perfect ecosystem, and we have everything we need from the earth to survive as well as improve our lives. Hasn't this been proven already?

As the most intelligent life forms on the planet, we should understand that our survival is in exact relation to our living planet. Human civilization is constantly growing.

If there is no unity, we will consume our planet's resources, and we will continue the same course of what is beginning to look like self-destruction. I am in opposition. I know our capabilities. We need purpose; we need unity.

Let's think big and begin small rather than thinking small and not beginning anything.

When families are united, this unity will spread to the community. When the community is united, it will spread to other communities. When communities are united, it will spread to a country. When a country is united, it will spread to other countries. This unity will continue until we are in a better world.

Now, let's think big and begin smaller. Self-love needs to be implemented. You need to believe in yourself. Know that you are not perfect, but most important, you are perfectly you. Your soul, your spirit, contains all the ingredients that make you. The first duty of your life is to love yourself; this is a necessity, and God demands that this

duty be fulfilled. It was already commanded of you at your miraculous birth.

I love myself. I know exactly who I am: I exist. I am here because God created me, and I know God loves me. I am his son of many sons and daughters. I am highly favored. I am LaMont Erik Carter. I am loved.

This knowledge is what makes me powerful. I know I have purpose, which shows I am a leader with particularly good information to complete a mission successfully.

I wrote this book for my brothers and sisters. I want you to know that your Faith, Salvation, Righteousness, Truth, Word, and Readiness are recognized. I want you to know that we are united. A movement does not need to be seen. A movement needs to be performed with actions and deeds. God demands this from us. We need effectiveness and efficiency.

I want you to have your happiness. I do not want you to sacrifice your spirit or the spark of it. I know you need

yourself fully intact. I will lead by example. I need you to know that I am in full alliance with you. Most important, I do not want you to simply follow me—I want you to follow my lead. There is a difference! I believe that leadership is situational. A new situation could require a new lead to follow. This is how we will become strong.

I have told you about my life experiences. I needed you to have this information. I need you to understand exactly who I am. Today, I will act. I will do honorable deeds. I am a soldier. I love life, and I want to live all my life to the fullest!

So let me begin.

I love all of my brothers and sisters. My relationship with them is what ignites my soul and spirit. I want all my brothers and sisters to believe in themselves. Your life is precious! I love you because you are still living it!

I have learned from you. I have learned what we are capable of being. I have experienced our love, hate, greed,

lust, and more. I know we still have a truth. It is the purpose of my existence to believe in you.

I believe that our lives and the freedom of it are protected by the fundamental fact that we are supposed to learn how to love our brothers and sisters. We got off course by distrusting each other, because we act like we do not have a direction, and we let anything guide us, especially if it involves money. Your love and all the love you have is your wealth. This is what you have of full value in any amount. In fact, I command you to secure this wealth ASAP. Brothers and sisters, we must fully understand our wealth. Therefore, I am requesting your allegiance.

I am a soldier of truth. I am under the full command of truth. I am an E-4 corporal. My commander let me keep my highest rank from service for my country, and I honor it! I willfully accept that I have word, truth, faith, righteousness, and salvation, and I am ready.

My mission is to make a better world. My commander

gave me the mission. I accepted willfully. I know I must accomplish this mission with objectives first.

You must believe that you are more than what you think.

The only way to accomplish this is learning how to love yourself. You will never be what you are meant to be if you do not love and accept yourself. Your life depends on this! You need to know that you are highly favored. It is impossible to have faith in your brothers and sisters if you do not have faith in yourself. Learning to love your brothers and sisters is initiated by loving yourself.

Know your faults and understand that you are not perfect. This will help you evaluate yourself in a way that will help you ascend. You will be better.

I believe in a man and woman relationship. The wealth of that union is a child. That child is the beginning of the creation of wealth for that man and woman, or king and queen!

Your kingdom is what you make it. This has everything to do with my commander and me!

My main objective is clearing the path. We have many obstacles in our way. I want to provide a clear path for my brothers and sisters to follow.

To my sisters, specifically queens and mothers: I am ashamed. I have been ignorant unintentionally, unworthy of your blessings. I have lied to you. I made you feel unimportant. I have been weak, so I made you weak. I let the conditions of the way life is being lived conquer me. I let these conditions influence my actions toward you. I was manipulated, so I manipulated you. I let our consistent struggle temporarily make me delusional. These are not the actions of a man or king. I want to clear these obstacles from our path.

I have regained my senses, my sisters. Now, I am strong and powerful. I know you are precious. I know you are

strong. I know you are intelligent. Most important, I know that you are the foundation of family. Life and the nurturing of it begins with you. I will not use my strength against you; I will use my strength for you, my sisters. We need order. We should not let our struggle continue to divert us from the path. Tomorrow is the future. The past has been set—it's done. You have a responsibility, my sisters, of the utmost importance. As I stated, you are the bringers of life. You need to reevaluate this precious ability and gift. You are valuable.

You are not meant to have children simply to spread life. You have a connection to your child. Your child learns love from you. You are on the front line of a better world because you have the ability and gift to create tomorrow. This is truth. You know the capability of God's children.

Therefore, let us act accordingly. You are creating and building a family, a kingdom. Take the necessary steps to ensure it has a strong foundation. You are in charge.

Stop looking at bank accounts and material assets as a foundation for your family. Look at our families today. They are broken because the necessary foundation for a strong family has not been applied. Having children out of wedlock is accepted in our society, but our society does not have a good benchmark. That is why we are in this predicament today. If you want a strong son or daughter, you will need to take the proper action. A father should be a man with honor. A father should be a provider. A father should have an ideal or effect that is beneficial for his family. He will be your king, and you will be his queen. This is simple. Kings and queens need to be in an agreement. There should not be any doubt! Your kingdoms success depends on this agreement.

You have worth, my sisters. You are intellectuals. You have an uncanny ability to gather information from different sources. Attempting to explain this ability would be tiresome. You are inquisitive. This is how you discover whether a king is worthy of a queen. I am constantly

telling you of your value because I need to you believe it. There are still brothers out there who are weak. They have not awoken. They will do to you as I have done before I gathered my strength. I need you to avoid them, my sisters. Wait until they regain their strength. You cannot help them. You could not help me. They will be susceptible to God's command only when they hear it.

You are the daughters of God.

I ask for your forgiveness, my queens.

I ask for your forgiveness, my sisters.

Join me, sisters. Help me complete my commander's mission and make this world better.

Sisters, I need you. You will create life, or you already have created life. I need you to regain your strength and your power as queens. Your children are the results of a union with a man. He is the child's father. It is your duty as queens to give your children everything they need to

be strong people. The love of a mother and father is a key element for making children begin to believe in themselves. How many instances of broken families lack this necessary foundation? Children are the future. The future is not promised to us individually. Any advantage or benefit a child has for making and surviving the future should be available at all cost.

Stop using society's benchmark as a guide for your children. God is the guide. God loves his children. God wants his children to have faith, character, and honor. God wants his children to receive all the love due to them for this accomplishment. Children should not be the victims of our past or present circumstances. Why should they be punished? The future is the gift and obstacle for our children. We need our children fully equipped to handle the creation of a better future.

If we initiate this ASAP, we will improve our chances for better, stronger families in the future. If you join me, I will demand this from you.

To my brothers: I want you to join me!

We have been at odds! We hurt each other and kill each other—for what, I do not know. I have not gain anything from opposing you. I was weak. I am strong and powerful now. I know exactly who you are and what you are capable of being.

You are my brother; I have learned from you. In a sense, you have been a father, uncle, brother, and cousin who became family (when we were not opposing each other). I have learned from our opposition, brothers. I have learned how base we have become. We have been belligerent and lackadaisical toward each other. This is unacceptable! Do you believe you are sons of God? Is this

what God commanded of you? No! You are meant to be soldiers of truth! You have faith, salvation, righteousness, truth, word, and readiness. If you are lacking, you cannot be what we are meant to be. I know this to be true. I have brothers who are in full allegiance with me—kings who share their kingdoms with me in full faith and trust. That is why I am strong and powerful. That is why I know I am highly favored.

I command you to understand this, brothers! You are highly favored. A falsified image of you has been presented! You have been weakened by the trials and struggles of life. You have been made to believe your wealth is monetary! Therefore, you can be led in any direction (think of a mule, and a carrot on a stick). Money or any monetary wealth is a nice tool to get things done, nothing more. The value of what you give is the value of what you receive. That is simply good business, which brings me to our duties!

Brothers, at our basic level, we are the creators of life. We need a bringer of life in order to create life. This is our instinct. Learn from God. Love what you create! Give that life everything it needs to survive. Give that life the opportunity to be strong and powerful. Give that life faith that it is precious. This will make you a king! Now, you are gaining your wealth. You will have a family!

Our sisters have been disrespected by us, brothers. Yes, it is because of what we suffered! We come from broken families. Yes, we are trying, brothers. I know this to be true. We need to succeed. This is how faith is gathered.

Let's begin from here, brothers!

Establish our honor and character. You will need to evaluate yourself. It may be difficult for you, but this is a necessity. You are a child of God! You are a son of God! You have the power.

We need to know where we stand with ourselves, brothers. This is how we overcome. This is how we

improve. Our families and kingdoms are not intact. It is our duty to get our families and kingdoms intact. We must understand our flaws. We need to know whether our flaws are imperfections or our own will and desire. We must understand we can improve. This is truth.

Brothers and kings, we cannot change how we are loved on this day. The results of our weaknesses have been validated. It is our strength that is relevant now. Our strength will bring honor to our character. We cannot control love. Love is not a possession. Love is not a greed. Love is not a lust. Love is not jealousy. Love is not hatred. Love is not fear. Love is only related to faith, loyalty, and honor. This is our character, brothers. This is how we was always meant to be. We are birthed with this dignity. This is how you are meant to be!

I am a king. The first duty as a king is to convince and show you that you are kings, brothers, if you do not know already. I want to be a king among kings. I know I cannot

rule you or your kingdom. I can only form a truthful alliance with you. I can only request your allegiance. If you accept, I will demand that you join me in making our world better! These are the actions of a king and brother. I need you to follow my lead. I am providing all the information that I have acquired through my experiences and training in life by God.

To my brothers and sisters: We need to have grace. We have fallen. Now, we will rise. We need to atone and repent. We have witnessed hatred. We have witnessed destruction of lives and cultures. We have witnessed wars. This is our past and present. Today, discrimination, hunger, poverty, and death still exist. We can change and prepare for tomorrow. Let us make tomorrow better. Let us unite our families honorably. Let us begin our ascension to a better world.

Brothers and sisters, gather what we have of our families. Yes, families are broken, but they are not beyond

repair. We still have a chance. We still have hope. Our most valuable possession are our children. Remember that they are tomorrow. They are of high spirit. Their readiness to change the world is glorious. Our children need to be guided properly. Our children need good examples of family. Our children need the love of their families. Most important, our children need love from their mothers and fathers.

To my African American brothers and sisters:

Our country is established by law and commonality for the pursuit of happiness for us all! We must have more faith in ourselves. I love you; I have faith in you. We have overcome many trials and tribulations, but there are more on the horizon. There is a cost for freedom, brothers and sisters. Truth wants its chosen people to bear witness. Truth wants us to ignite our spirits and souls and choose to stand facing God as his soldiers under his full command. We

should not deny ourselves this righteousness. Our ancestors were slaves in our country. They survived the trials and tribulations of losing their dignity, honor, families, faith, culture, and past knowledge of ancestry. We are strong, brothers and sisters. But are we 14 percent of the population in our country strong? Are we still losing our dignity, honor, families, faith, culture, and knowledge? We must unite to save our children. We are not victims of God. We should learn from our past. We have adaptability. We have enough knowledge and experience to get back on the path of our destiny. We are sons and daughters of God. We are highly favored.

To my family: Mother, you are my queen. You are strong, wise, nurturing, and protective. Through you, I was birthed to this world. My life depended on you. Everything I am is because of God through you. Your son is strong and powerful. I will love you for the rest of my life. Mother,

I need your allegiance to complete my mission. Your grandchildren will need your wisdom and love to properly prepare them for the future intended for them by God. You are the bringer of life. Your love is an intricate part of the foundation for our family. Mother, you are a highly favored daughter of God.

Father, you are my king. Your son is strong and powerful. Through you, God created me. You protected me while I was becoming a man. Your love has been measured as truth by God through me. I still need you, Father. I need your allegiance. I am completing a mission that you initiated. Father, you are a highly favored son of God.

Brother, you are a king. You are strong and powerful. Your loyalty and faith in me are undeniable. Your ability to maintain your kingdom signifies your strength. I know your love; it is one of the many blessings God has given to me. Brother, you are a highly favored son of God.

Sister, you are a queen. Your kingdom is intact. You have survived all attacks of your faith. You have made yourself stronger. I feel the strength of your love. I will always be your protector. You are a mother. You are a bringer of life. Your sympathy and empathy for others are blessings to me from God. Sister, you are a highly favored daughter of God.

Soldiers, understand. I am committed. My faith is that God will grant me favor. Nothing is more glorious or victorious. Follow me. Gather your faith. Understand that salvation is achievable. Use the gifts and blessings that God has given you. Cleanse yourself of your sins. Tomorrow is a new day for days to come. Act! Our world will get better.

Here is my plan.

I will free at least two hundred of my brothers and sisters.

I will be a founder of two private foundations dedicated to making the world a better place.

I will strengthen family bonds.

These are not listed in an order. These are the tasks I must accomplish to complete my mission.

Freedom for at least two hundred of my brothers and sisters

Freedom is the ability to create your own kingdom, your truth. With freedom, you can naturally become self-aware. This is part of self-love. When your freedom is hindered or restrained in any way, it disrupts this natural ability.

I am not referring to the freedom and rights we have in our country. I am referring to the freedom within ourselves.

Once accomplished, I will have recruited soldiers of their own free will. The first task I will assign to them will be to follow my plan, detailed later. It is my faith and belief that once this task is completed, it will create stronger family bonds for my brothers and sisters.

I will be a founder and CEO of two private foundations and nonprofit corporations dedicated to making the world a better place.

I will start these two private foundations simultaneously.

The first will be a family foundation, and the second will be a nonprofit publishing corporation. Both foundations will have the same business plan structure with obvious differences based on the corporation. For example, the family foundation will repair and build stronger family bonds. I will start a legacy for my family. We will have recorded documented history of our participation in

making the world better. This will make progress toward building a stronger unity for African American families in the United States of America.

The nonprofit publishing corporation will build stronger communities. This will make progress toward creating a strong country. It is my belief that when we strengthen communities, they will expand to our country.

Both corporations' sole purpose is to make the world better.

Business Plan

Executive Summary

BWM Publishing Foundation has one purpose: to make the world a better place.

BWM Publishing will focus on health care, education, and employment.

BWM Publishing will target everyone in the world.

BWM Publishing will initially use its only product as a source of funding and getting operational.

BWM Publishing will initially use the internet to distribute its product. Initially, marketing will be by word of mouth by board members and shareholders (which will be anyone who purchases the product).

BWM Publishing welcomes and encourages competitors. Our company thrives off competition.

BWM Publishing is being built from the ground up. For the next three years, BWM will establish structure.

During the first three years of establishment, funds from product will be utilized during this process. Owners and staff will be selected. Business operational procedures and documentation will be completed. Business physical location will be determined.

BWM will be fully operational two years after establishment.

URL: BWMPUBLISHINGFOUNDATION.COM

Business Description

BWM Publishing Foundations sole purpose is to make the world a better place. The issues and problems that will be our primary goal to solve are discrimination, war, hunger, poverty, health care, employment, and religious conflicts. These are in the exact order of priority. Our company believes discrimination causes war. Hunger and poverty, poor health care, and religious conflicts are the result. Our company will target all the people in the world as buyers for our product.

Competitive Analysis

BWM Publishing will support all competitors. The NPC encourages competitiveness in this market. Corporations that are dedicated to making the world better will be allies.

Sales and Marketing Plan

BWM Publishing's product is this book. This book contains the CEO and founder's resume and his initial blueprint for achieving our goals. Our product will cost twenty US dollars. During the first year, all corporation employees will be the sales and marketing department. The funds will be the initial investment for our corporation's prosperity and success.

Ownership and Management Plan

BWM Publishing is a start-up. We will create a strong foundation. Our product is not just a book; it is an ideal and plan that needs to be distributed to all my brothers and sisters who oppose self-destruction of our planet and ourselves.

Shareholders, board members, and staffing assignments will be completed approximately one year after product launch. The prediction for salaries will be as follows.

All executive salaries will be equal and limited to one hundred thousand dollars yearly. Based on my research, this is on the exceptionally low end of executive salaries. The reason is simple: we are not doing this for monetary gain. We are here because we are under the command of truth.

All other staffing, directors, and managers have salaries that will be determined based on skill, experience, and profession after our company structure is more established.

Operating Plan

Six months to a year after starting, BWM Publishing will be generating funds via sales of product. These funds will be needed to establish both corporations (BWM Publishing Foundation and OFL Private Foundation). After both Corporations have been established, a more refined, concise business plan will be developed using this blueprint. However, there will be modifications and effective additions to target the companies' objectives to complete our mission.

We will develop standard operating procedures and determine a physical location for both companies.

After all assignments and positions have been filled, these tasks will be assigned to individuals or groups to be successfully completed.

Financial Plan

All start-up costs will be provided by founder and CEO, as well as product sales during the first year of establishment.

BWM Publishing Foundation will be 100 percent transparent. It will allow buyers of our product to automatically become shareholders, and they will be able to view documented company actions via the internet and logon credentials, which will be created during purchasing of product.

This is my plan to accomplish the mission truth has assigned to me.

I am LaMont Erik Carter. I am the Son of God. I Believe that life is the most precious thing on Earth. My life has been victorious and glorious since my miraculous birth. I was the first born of my virgin Mother.

My family were rejoiced at my birth because they knew I was sent by God. I have achieved many victories over struggle and suffering throughout my life. This is how I was measured by God to ensure I was ready. This is Truth.

This is my Truth:

When I walked on earth as a man, I was crucified. As a man, I was attacked by all variations of temptation and was victorious. As a man, I was able to protect myself from allowing hate and greed to hinder my spiritual connection to God. After these accomplishments came my glory. God sent for me. I ascended, and my spirit was called to God. God gave me forgiveness for all my earthly sins and

commanded me to fall under the command of Truth. I want to tell you this. When God commanded me to stand under truth's command, he granted me strength and power through truth. I requested that my strength be Love and that my power be Faith.

My Faith:

My Faith is the most powerful weapon I utilize as a Soldier of Truth. I have Faith that I will inherit the Kingdom of Heaven that God has gifted to me. I have Faith that my brothers and sisters will know who I am. I have Faith that I will successfully accomplish my mission to make the World better.

My Salvation:

My Salvation is evident. Despite all attacks on my mind, body and soul, I am still here. I have forgiven myself for all my sins. I still have my Truth and my Faith.

My Righteousness:

I am the Son of God. It is my duty to preserve the Kingdom of Heaven with all my strength and power.

I am Ready. I want a glorious victory. Victory will only be measured as the uplifting of spirits. Life will be preserved at all costs.

Printed in the United States
By Bookmasters